From "Me" To "We"

THE 30-DAY WORKBOOK

Your Daily Practice for Building a Shared Language
in Your Relationship

A Companion to the Marriage Communication
Guide for New Couples

ERIC A. WILLIAMS, PhD.

WWW.TRUEVINEPUBLISHING.ORG

From "Me" To "We"
Eric A. Williams, PhD.

Published by
True Vine Publishing Co.
810 Dominican Dr.
Nashville, TN 37228
www.TrueVinePublishing.org

Scripture quotations taken from The Holy Bible, New International Version® NIV®

Copyright © 1973, 1978, 1984, 2011 by Biblica, Inc. Used with permission. All rights reserved worldwide.

ISBN: 978-1-968092-41-2 Paperback
ISBN: 978-1-968092-42-9 eBook

Printed in the United States—First printing

DEDICATION

To the brave couples that truly believe their marriage is their most important investment and desire to "win in marriage" and defy the narrative fifty percent of marriages end in divorce applies to them. To those who understand that love is not a destination, but a daily conversation.

This work is dedicated to those who choose to drop their armor, pick up a pen, and commit to the intentional, often challenging, but always rewarding journey of building a shared language through vulnerability and transparency. May the courage you show in these pages become the bedrock of your family's legacy.

Workbook Methodology:
Your Blueprint for Action

Congratulations on taking the courageous step to dedicate 30 days to strengthening your marriage communication!

This workbook is your training field—the place where the principles of effective communication are forged into daily habits. But every great construction needs a blueprint.

The Essential Connection: Theory Meets Practice

This 30-Day Workbook is the hands-on companion to my core book, *Marriage Communication Guide for New Couples: From "Me" to "We"*. Think of them this way:

- The Main Book (The Blueprint): This is where you learn the *theory*— the what and why. It explains the root causes of conflict, details the family-of-origin blueprints that shape your communication, and provides the psychological and relational science behind effective change. Without the blueprint, the practice lacks depth.

- This Workbook (The Daily Build): This is where you master the *skill*— the how and when. It converts the powerful concepts from the main book (like understanding the "Effective Arrow" and the 5 Apology Languages) into small, measurable, and mandatory daily actions. Without the daily build, the blueprint remains just a theory. Each daily "**Snippet from 'Me to We**" is followed by the chapter number in parentheses so you can revisit the corresponding chapter in the main book.

If you have already read the *Marriage Communication Guide*, you are perfectly equipped to dive in. If you haven't, I strongly recommend acquiring the main book. It will give you the foundational knowledge needed to unlock the deepest value of these exercises.

How to Use This Workbook Daily

We designed each day's entry for maximal relational impact with minimal time commitment (15–20 minutes). Consistency is the key to success.

1. Read the Lesson (5 minutes): Start by reading the "**DAILY LESSON**", the "**THOUGHT-PROVOKING QUOTE**", and the "**SOURCE OF WISDOM".** This sets the necessary mental and emotional context for the day's theme.

2. Do the Work (10–15 minutes): This is the core reciprocal exercise. Follow the steps under "**THE WORK**", ensuring both partners participate honestly and write down their responses. This is the negotiation, the discussion, and the commitment.

3. Reflect and Commit: Use the **Reflection Space** to note your individual and shared takeaways. The commitment you write down should be clear and actionable in the next 24 hours.

Crucial Note: This is a workbook for two. Commit to completing the daily task together, or at least discussing your written responses with one another before the end of the day. The journey from "Me" to "We" is built one shared conversation at a time.

WEEK 1: THE "ME" FACTOR (UNDERSTANDING MY COMMUNICATION BLUEPRINT)

DAY 1: BEYOND "ME" TO "WE"

DAILY LESSON

DAY 1: BEYOND "ME" TO "WE"

Snippet from "Me to We" (Chp 1): Effective communication between couples allows for the sharing of thoughts, emotions, desires, and needs. The answer lies in the individual communication styles, needs, and expectations that each person brings to the table, otherwise known as the **"Me"**.

THOUGHT-PROVOKING QUOTE: "A great marriage is not when the 'perfect couple' comes together. It is when an imperfect couple learns to enjoy their differences." — *Dave Meurer*

SOURCE OF WISDOM: Genesis 2:24 (NIV): "That is why a man leaves his father and mother and is united to his wife, and they become one flesh."

THE WORK: Our Mutual Reward Contract

GOAL: Establish the positive incentive that will power you through the next 30 days as a unified team.

1. The Promise: Individually, and *without sharing*, write down one specific, memorable reward you will commit to giving your partner if and only if you both complete all 30 days of the workbook. (Must be something you truly believe your partner would enjoy.)

2. The Contract: Write down your commitment below, sign and date it, but **DO NOT REVEAL THE REWARD** to your partner.

3. The Seal: On a separate sheet of paper, write out the reward you are committing to your partner and seal it in an envelope. You will open it on Day 30. This sealed commitment is your mutual contract.

REFLECTION SPACE

My Signed Commitment (Partner A):

I, _____, promise to deliver the sealed reward to my partner upon the completion of Day 30.

Signature _____ Date _____

My Signed Commitment (Partner B):

I, _____, promise to deliver the sealed reward to my partner upon the completion of Day 30.

Signature _____ Date _____

DAY 2: THE FAMILY BLUEPRINT

DAILY LESSON

DAY 2: THE FAMILY BLUEPRINT

Snippet from "Me to We" (Chp 1): Our family and upbringing have a big impact on how we communicate. These early experiences shape our basic values, like what's right or wrong, how to show love and loyalty, and what responsibilities we have.

THOUGHT-PROVOKING QUOTE: "You get what you tolerate. You get what you model. You get what you reinforce." — *Dr. Henry Cloud*

SOURCE OF WISDOM: Proverbs 22:6 (NIV): "Start children off on the way they should go, and even when they are old they will not turn from it."

THE WORK: Map It: Our Communication Heritage

GOAL: Uncover the unconscious communication habits you both inherited from your families of origin.

1. **Map It:** Both partners individually chart 3 distinct communication "rules" or habits learned from their family of origin (e.g., "We yell when stressed," "We avoid conflict at all costs," "We use sarcasm to express pain").

2. **The Impact:** Discuss the *feeling* your partner's top family rule triggers in you.

3. **The Upgrade:** Discuss and agree on one mutual communication rule you can both agree to retire from your marriage starting today.

REFLECTION SPACE

My 3 Family Rules (Partner A):

_____

_____

_____

_____

My 3 Family Rules (Partner B):

_____

_____

_____

_____

The Feeling Partner B's Rule Triggers in Me (Partner A writes):

_____

_____

_____

_____

The Feeling Partner A's Rule Triggers in Me (Partner B writes):

_____

_____

_____

_____

Our Shared Takeaway (Rule to Retire):

_____

_____

_____

_____

DAY 3: NEEDS VS. WANTS

DAILY LESSON

DAY 3: NEEDS VS. WANTS

Snippet from "Me to We" (Chp 1): Underlying our communication styles are a host of unspoken needs and desires that drive our interactions with our partners. These needs encompass a broad spectrum, ranging from the human yearning for connection and belonging to the more specific desires for validation, recognition, and affirmation.

THOUGHT-PROVOKING QUOTE: "Love is not simply a matter of what you do, but what you *need* to do in order to be whole." — *Gary Chapman*

SOURCE OF WISDOM: Philippians 4:19 (NIV): "And my God will meet all your needs according to the riches of his glory in Christ Jesus."

THE WORK: Listing Our Core Needs

GOAL: Clearly articulate your top three emotional needs and make an actionable, reciprocal commitment to meet one of your partner's needs.

1. **Identify & Discuss:** Both partners must independently list their top 3 core emotional needs. Once written, share and discuss: *Which need is the most urgent for you right now?*

2. **The Commitment:** Based on your discussion, both partners will write down one specific, small way they will try to meet the other partner's *most urgent* need in the next 48 hours.

REFLECTION SPACE

My 3 Core Emotional Needs (Partner A):

_____

_____

_____

_____

My 3 Core Emotional Needs (Partner B):

_____

_____

_____

_____

My Commitment to Partner B (Partner A writes):

_____

_____

_____

_____

My Commitment to Partner A (Partner B writes):

_____

_____

_____

_____

DAY 4: MY HIDDEN EXPECTATIONS

DAILY LESSON

DAY 4: MY HIDDEN EXPECTATIONS

Snippet from "Me to We" (Chp 1): Along with communication styles and needs, couples also bring a set of expectations that shape their interactions with their partner. Unrealistic or uncommunicated expectations can sow seeds of discord and resentment, undermining the emotional bond between us and our partner.

THOUGHT-PROVOKING QUOTE: "Resentment is like drinking poison and waiting for the other person to die." — *St. Augustine*

SOURCE OF WISDOM: Proverbs 3:5-6 (NIV): "Trust in the Lord with all your heart and lean not on your own understanding; in all your ways submit to him, and he will make your paths straight."

THE WORK: Unpacking the Hidden

GOAL: Both partners bring one uncommunicated expectation into the light and convert it into a direct, healthy request.

1. **Unpack:** Both partners write down one *uncommunicated* expectation they have (e.g., "They should anticipate my stress without me asking").

2. **The Consequence:** Both partners write down the emotional reaction they have when this expectation goes unmet (e.g., "I feel ignored," "I withdraw").

3. **Rephrase:** Rephrase the expectation as a clear, loving, and actionable direct request that you share and agree to honor.

REFLECTION SPACE

My Hidden Expectation (Partner A):

_____

_____

_____

_____

My Hidden Expectation (Partner B):

_____

_____

_____

_____

My Direct Request (The New Rule) (Partner A):

_____

_____

_____

_____

My Direct Request (The New Rule) (Partner B):

_____

_____

_____

_____

DAY 5: THE THREE ARROWS

DAILY LESSON

DAY 5: THE THREE ARROWS

Snippet from "Me to We" (Chp 2): Imagine communication as an arrow aimed at a target. Effective communication hits the bullseye with precision and accuracy, achieving its intended goal. Poor communication not only misses the target entirely but also causes collateral damage along the way.

THOUGHT-PROVOKING QUOTE: "We are experts on what we *meant* to say, but others are experts on what they *heard*." — *Dr. Harriet Lerner*

SOURCE OF WISDOM: Proverbs 18:21 (NIV): "The tongue has the power of life and death, and those who love it will eat its fruit."

THE WORK: Assessing Our Aim (Reciprocal)

GOAL: Reciprocally assess the communication "Arrow" used during recent conflict and commit to aiming for the Effective Arrow.

1. **Assess (A to B):** Partner A describes a recent disagreement. Partner B, using the terms from the lesson, assesses the "Arrow" Partner A used and why.

2. **Assess (B to A):** Partner B describes a recent disagreement. Partner A assesses the "Arrow" Partner B used and why.

3. **The Upgrade:** Discuss which arrow you both believe you most frequently use when frustrated and jointly identify one specific change that will help you aim for the Effective Arrow next time.

REFLECTION SPACE

My Assessment of Partner B's Arrow (Partner A writes):

_____

_____

_____

_____

My Assessment of Partner A's Arrow (Partner B writes):

_____

_____

_____

_____

My Dominant Arrow (Self-Assessment) (Partner A):

_____

_____

_____

_____

My Dominant Arrow (Self-Assessment) (Partner B):

_____

_____

_____

_____

Our Shared Takeaway (Upgrade Plan):

_____

_____

DAY 6: "ALL-OR-NOTHING" TRAPS

DAILY LESSON

DAY 6: "ALL-OR-NOTHING" TRAPS

Snippet from "Me to We" (Chp 9): Phrases like "you always..." or "you never..." are examples of this form of speech. These toxic phrases put the other person on defense and discredits any good qualities they have all because of the one frustration at hand.

THOUGHT-PROVOKING QUOTE: "Speak your truth clearly and assertively. Do not allow anyone to diminish your voice." — *Iyanla Vanzant*

SOURCE OF WISDOM: Ephesians 4:29 (NIV): "Do not let any unwholesome talk come out of your mouths, but only what is helpful for building others up according to their needs, that it may benefit those who listen."

THE WORK: The "I" Statement Challenge

GOAL: Both partners practice expressing feelings and needs without using global attacks that undermine their partner's character.

1. **Identify:** Both partners individually write down one "All-or-Nothing" phrase they either use or frequently hear from their partner (e.g., "You *never* help with the kids!").

2. **The Rewrite:** Both partners rephrase their toxic phrase into a constructive "I" statement that expresses their feeling, the situation, and their need.

3. **The Discussion:** Share your "I" statements. Discuss how the new phrasing changes the *mood* of the conversation and commit to using it going forward.

REFLECTION SPACE

My Toxic Phrase (Partner A):

_____

_____

_____

_____

My Toxic Phrase (Partner B):

_____

_____

_____

_____

The "I" Statement Rewrite (Partner A):

_____

_____

_____

_____

The "I" Statement Rewrite (Partner B):

_____

_____

_____

_____

Our Shared Takeaway (Commitment to "I" Statements):

_____

_____

DAY 7: WEEK 1 REVIEW & GOAL SETTING

DAILY LESSON

DAY 7: WEEK 1 REVIEW & GOAL SETTING

Snippet from "Me to We" (Chp 1): Being conscious of our expectations allows us to recognize the influence our expectations may have over us and make informed adjustments when necessary. Through reflection, dialogue, and mutual respect, we can develop communication practices that honor the unique perspectives and needs of each partner.

THOUGHT-PROVOKING QUOTE: "Self-knowledge is the first step to self-correction." — *Unknown*

SOURCE OF WISDOM: Romans 12:2 (NIV): "Do not conform to the pattern of this world, but be transformed by the renewing of your mind."

THE WORK: The "Me" Audit and "We" Focus

GOAL: Summarize your individual lessons from Week 1 and set a unified goal for understanding your partner's *languages* in Week 2.

1. **The "Me" Audit:** Both partners individually discuss one thing they learned about their *own* communication style, needs, or expectations this week that they didn't fully realize before.

2. **The "We" Focus:** Both partners write down how this new self-knowledge changes how they will listen to their partner.

3. **The Goal:** Set one shared communication goal for Week 2 (e.g., "We will intentionally observe each other's Love Language every day").

REFLECTION SPACE

My Biggest Week 1 Realization (Partner A):

_____

_____

_____

_____

My Biggest Week 1 Realization (Partner B):

_____

_____

_____

_____

How I will Listen Differently (Partner A):

_____

_____

_____

_____

How I will Listen Differently (Partner B):

_____

_____

_____

_____

Our Week 2 Shared Goal:

_____

_____

WEEK 2: DECODING OUR LANGUAGES (LOVE, APOLOGY, AND STYLE)

DAY 8: MY PRIMARY LOVE LANGUAGE

DAILY LESSON

DAY 8: MY PRIMARY LOVE LANGUAGE

Snippet from "Me to We" (Chp 3): For those unfamiliar with the term Love Language, it's a concept introduced by Dr. Gary Chapman in his widely acclaimed book *The 5 Love Languages*. Everyone has a primary Love Language, a specific channel through which they feel most cherished and valued.

THOUGHT-PROVOKING QUOTE: "The greatest need in the human heart is the need to be loved unconditionally, to be affirmed, and to be valued." — *Gary Chapman*

SOURCE OF WISDOM: 1 John 4:19 (NIV): "We love because he first loved us."

THE WORK: The Language Gap (Reciprocal)

GOAL: Both partners confirm their Love Language, identify where a recent effort missed the mark, and commit to improving.

1. **Share:** Both partners clearly state their primary Love Language.

2. **The Gap:** Both partners describe a time this year when their partner showed love using a *different* language when they really craved their own. How did it feel?

3. **The Fix:** Both partners write one specific way they will ensure their next effort lands correctly.

REFLECTION SPACE

My top LL(s) and What makes it/them so significant to me (Partner A):

_____

_____

_____

_____

My top LL(s) and What makes it/them so significant to me (Partner B):

_____

_____

_____

_____

The Communication Gap Example (Partner A):

_____

_____

_____

_____

The Communication Gap Example (Partner B):

_____

_____

_____

_____

Our Shared Takeaway (My Commitment to _Their_ LL):

_____

_____

DAY 9: SPEAKING THEIR LOVE LANGUAGE

DAY 9: SPEAKING THEIR LOVE LANGUAGE

Snippet from "Me to We" (Chp 3): When you are able to communicate to your partner the ways that you prefer to receive love and apologies, they can meet your needs better than if they were to try to guess. These languages act as a roadmap for couples to better comprehend and communicate their emotional needs.

THOUGHT-PROVOKING QUOTE: "Love isn't a feeling; it's a practice." — *M. Scott Peck*

SOURCE OF WISDOM: Mark 10:45 (NIV): "For even the Son of Man did not come to be served, but to serve, and to give his life as a ransom for many."

THE WORK: Intentional Practice

GOAL: Both partners apply intentional effort to serve their partner using their specific Love Language today and report on the emotional impact.

1. **The Act:** Both partners commit to one small, intentional act today that aligns *perfectly* with their partner's primary Love Language.

2. **The Report:** Both partners write down the emotional impact of the *act they received*. Then, both discuss how it felt to intentionally *give* love in a way that wasn't their default.

3. **The Score:** Rate the emotional connection on a scale of 1-10 for the day.

REFLECTION SPACE

My Intentional LL Act Given to Partner B (Partner A writes):

_____

_____

_____

_____

My Intentional LL Act Given to Partner A (Partner B writes):

_____

_____

_____

_____

My Emotional Reaction to the Act I Received (Partner A):

_____

_____

_____

_____

My Emotional Reaction to the Act I Received (Partner B):

_____

_____

_____

_____

Our Shared Takeaway (Connection Score):

_____

_____

DAY 10: MY APOLOGY STYLE

DAILY LESSON

DAY 10: MY APOLOGY STYLE

Snippet from "Me to We" (Chp 3): When you are able to communicate to your partner the ways that you prefer to receive love and apologies, they can meet your needs better than if they were to try to guess.

THOUGHT-PROVOKING QUOTE: "Apologizing is not a sign of weakness; it's a commitment to the relationship." — *Unknown*

SOURCE OF WISDOM: Psalm 51:17 (NIV): "The sacrifices of God are a broken spirit; a broken and contrite heart, O God, you will not despise."

THE WORK: The Anatomy of Our Apologies

GOAL: Both partners identify their natural apology style and commit to integrating the Accepting Responsibility language.

1. **Identify:** Individually, write a brief apology for a common mistake (e.g., forgetting a small chore). Analyze which of the 5 Apology Languages (from "Me to We" book) you naturally lean toward.

2. **Exchange & Review:** Exchange your written apologies. Both partners identify which Apology Language their partner used and discuss if it felt satisfying.

3. **The Goal:** Both partners commit to intentionally integrating the Accepting Responsibility language into their next apology.

REFLECTION SPACE

My Natural Apology Style (Partner A):

_____

_____

_____

_____

My Natural Apology Style (Partner B):

_____

_____

_____

_____

My Partner's Review (Satisfying? Why/Why not?) (Partner A writes):

_____

_____

_____

_____

My Partner's Review (Satisfying? Why/Why not?) (Partner B writes):

_____

_____

_____

_____

Our Shared Takeaway (Goal for Responsibility Language):

_____

_____

DAY 11: RECEIVING A SINCERE APOLOGY

DAILY LESSON

DAY 11: RECEIVING A SINCERE APOLOGY

Snippet from "Me to We" (Chp 9): To address issues and develop effective connections becomes impossible when one partner shuts down. Toxic language can vary; even jokes have the power to negatively impact the trust in a relationship.

THOUGHT-PROVOKING QUOTE: "To err is human, to forgive, divine." — *Alexander Pope*

SOURCE OF WISDOM: Colossians 3:13 (NIV): "Bear with each other and forgive one another if any of you has a grievance against someone. Forgive as the Lord forgave you."

THE WORK: Defining "Sincere"

GOAL: Both partners define what a genuine repair attempt looks and feels like to them, allowing the other to meet that need.

1. **Teach:** Both partners explain to the other what a true, sincere apology looks and feels like to them (words, tone, changed behavior, etc.).

2. **The Repair Attempt:** Both partners describe a past argument where the apology felt only *superficial*. What was the one element that was missing?

3. **The Agreement:** Agree on a phrase your partner can use when an apology feels incomplete (e.g., "I need a deeper repair on that one").

REFLECTION SPACE

My Definition of a Sincere Apology (Partner A):

_____

_____

_____

_____

My Definition of a Sincere Apology (Partner B):

_____

_____

_____

_____

The Missing Element in a Past Argument (Partner A):

_____

_____

_____

_____

The Missing Element in a Past Argument (Partner B):

_____

_____

_____

_____

Our Shared Takeaway (Agreement Phrase):

_____

_____

DAY 12: PASSIVE VS. ASSERTIVE

DAILY LESSON

DAY 12: PASSIVE VS. ASSERTIVE

Snippet from "Me to We" (Chp 2): Understanding your partner's communication style begins with paying attention to their verbal cues, which can offer valuable insights into their thoughts. Some may gravitate towards direct and assertive forms of communication, while others may lean towards a more indirect and passive approach.

THOUGHT-PROVOKING QUOTE: "Your problem is you're too busy holding onto your unworthiness." — *Ram Dass*

SOURCE OF WISDOM: Ephesians 4:15 (NIV): "Instead, speaking the truth in love, we will grow to become in every respect the mature body of him who is the head, that is, Christ."

THE WORK: Assertiveness in Practice (Reciprocal)

GOAL: Both partners practice asserting a need clearly and respectfully, shifting away from passive or aggressive communication.

1. **Style Check:** Both partners identify one moment this week where they felt Passive (didn't speak up) and one where they felt Aggressive (spoke too harshly).

2. **The Rewrite:** Both partners take the passive moment and rephrase their entire communication using a clear, respectful "I" Statement to assert their original need.

3. **The Practice:** Share the rewritten assertive statements. Discuss the difference in how you *feel* when hearing the assertive version versus the memory of the original moment.

REFLECTION SPACE

My Assertive Rewrite (Partner A):

_____

_____

_____

_____

My Assertive Rewrite (Partner B):

_____

_____

_____

_____

My Feeling after Hearing Partner B's Shift (Partner A writes):

_____

_____

_____

_____

My Feeling after Hearing Partner A's Shift (Partner B writes):

_____

_____

_____

_____

Our Shared Takeaway (Plan to use "I" statements):

_____

_____

DAY 13: NON-VERBAL CUES

DAY 13: NON-VERBAL CUES

Snippet from "Me to We" (Chp 4): When it comes to active listening, you focus not only on the words spoken but also on the emotions and intentions behind them. By validating their feelings and experiences, you deepen your emotional bond and enhance your communication skills as a couple.

THOUGHT-PROVOKING QUOTE: "The most important thing in communication is hearing what isn't said." — *Peter Drucker*

SOURCE OF WISDOM: Proverbs 4:23 (NIV): "Above all else, guard your heart, for everything you do flows from it."

THE WORK: Silent Signals (Reciprocal)

GOAL: Practice observation and decoding the unspoken language of the body and tone through reciprocal observation.

1. **Observe (Round 1):** Partner A speaks for 3 minutes about a neutral topic. Partner B silently notes their non-verbal cues. Partner B reports back what they observed and what they interpreted it to mean.

2. **Observe (Round 2):** Swap roles. Partner B speaks for 3 minutes. Partner A observes, decodes, and reports back.

3. **Confirm:** Both partners confirm the accuracy of the reading and discuss which non-verbal cue is the most dominant and honest signal in your marriage.

REFLECTION SPACE

My Dominant Non-Verbal Cue (My Partner observed this) (Partner A):

_____

_____

_____

_____

My Dominant Non-Verbal Cue (My Partner observed this) (Partner B):

_____

_____

_____

_____

My Interpretation of Partner A's Internal State (Partner B writes):

_____

_____

_____

_____

My Interpretation of Partner B's Internal State (Partner A writes):

_____

_____

_____

_____

Our Shared Takeaway (The Most Honest Signal):

_____

_____

DAY 14: WEEK 2 REVIEW & GOAL SETTING

DAILY LESSON

DAY 14: WEEK 2 REVIEW & GOAL SETTING

Snippet from "Me to We" (Chp 4): Actively listening to your partner demonstrates respect and empathy, creating a safe space for them to express themselves authentically. Your willingness to be vulnerable and honest fosters trust and strengthens your emotional connection with your partner.

THOUGHT-PROVOKING QUOTE: "Appreciation is the highest form of prayer, for it acknowledges the presence of good wherever we shine the light of our thankful thoughts." — *Alan Cohen*

SOURCE OF WISDOM: 1 Thessalonians 5:18 (NIV): "Give thanks in all circumstances; for this is God's will for you in Christ Jesus."

THE WORK: The Appreciation Jar & The "We" Goal

GOAL: Cement the lessons of Week 2 by focusing on gratitude and setting a goal for building your shared language.

1. **Appreciation Jar:** Both partners individually write down three specific ways their partner demonstrated understanding of their "languages" (Love or Apology) this week.

2. **Read Aloud:** Read them to your partner.

3. **The Goal:** Discuss and set one shared communication goal for Week 3: Crafting Our "We" (e.g., "We will define one common word that causes confusion").

REFLECTION SPACE

3 Ways My Partner Showed Understanding (Partner A):

_____

_____

_____

_____

3 Ways My Partner Showed Understanding (Partner B):

_____

_____

_____

_____

My Feeling about Receiving Appreciation (Partner A):

_____

_____

_____

_____

My Feeling about Receiving Appreciation (Partner B):

_____

_____

_____

_____

Our Week 3 Shared Goal:

_____

_____

WEEK 3: CRAFTING OUR "WE" (BUILDING THE SHARED LANGUAGE)

DAY 15: COMMON TERMINOLOGY

DAILY LESSON

DAY 15: COMMON TERMINOLOGY

Snippet from "Me to We" (Chp 5): Effective communication requires the establishment of a shared language, a common framework of terms, methods, norms, and boundaries that enables clear and meaningful interaction. This process involves open dialogue, active listening, and mutual respect.

THOUGHT-PROVOKING QUOTE: "If two people agree on everything, one of them is unnecessary." — *Winston Churchill*

SOURCE OF WISDOM: 1 Corinthians 1:10 (NIV): "I appeal to you, brothers and sisters, in the name of our Lord Jesus Christ, that all of you agree with one another in what you say and that there be no divisions among you, but that you be perfectly united in mind and thought."

THE WORK: Defining Our Dictionary

GOAL: Negotiate and agree on precise, shared definitions for two words that often lead to miscommunication.

1. **Identify:** List two words or phrases that have consistently caused confusion in your marriage (e.g., "Be here soon," "Clean the house," "A good date night").

2. **Define:** For Term 1, write down your individual definitions.

3. **Agree:** Negotiate and write down one precise, shared definition for Term 1 that you both commit to using moving forward.

REFLECTION SPACE

Term 1 & My Definition (Partner A):

_____

_____

_____

_____

Term 1 & My Definition (Partner B):

_____

_____

_____

_____

Term 2 & My Definition (Partner A):

_____

_____

_____

_____

Term 2 & My Definition (Partner B):

_____

_____

_____

_____

Our Shared Definition for Term 1:

_____

_____

DAY 16: ACTIVE LISTENING MASTERY

DAILY LESSON

DAY 16: ACTIVE LISTENING MASTERY

Snippet from "Me to We" (Chp 4): It's not simply about hearing words but actively working to understand the other person's perspective through those words. By practicing active listening, you create a space where the other person feels valued and heard, fostering a deeper connection and making communication more meaningful.

THOUGHT-PROVOKING QUOTE: "The most precious gift we can offer others is our presence. When mindfulness embraces those we love, they will bloom like flowers." — *Thích Nhất Hạnh*

SOURCE OF WISDOM: James 1:19 (NIV): "My dear brothers and sisters, take note of this: Everyone should be quick to listen, slow to speak and slow to become angry."

THE WORK: The 3-Minute Mirror (Reciprocal)

GOAL: Practice the core skill of reflective listening to ensure comprehension before response through a reciprocal exercise.

1. **Round 1:** Partner A speaks for exactly 3 minutes on a recent challenge or feeling they experienced. Partner B must then reflect back (paraphrase) exactly what they heard, ensuring the emotional content is captured.

2. **Round 2:** Swap roles. Partner B speaks for 3 minutes. Partner A reflects back.

3. **The Validation:** Both partners write about their success in reflection.

REFLECTION SPACE

Partner A's Feeling Shared (Partner A writes):

_____

_____

_____

_____

Partner B's Feeling Shared (Partner B writes):

_____

_____

_____

_____

My Success at Reflective Listening (Partner A writes about Partner B's Reflection):

_____

_____

_____

_____

My Success at Reflective Listening (Partner B writes about Partner A's Reflection):

_____

_____

_____

_____

Our Shared Takeaway (How it felt to be fully heard):

_____

_____

DAY 17: BOUNDARY SETTING 101

DAILY LESSON

DAY 17: BOUNDARY SETTING 101

Snippet from "Me to We" (Chp 5): You and your partner may also need to discuss boundaries around certain topics or behaviors to ensure that both parties feel safe and respected within the relationship. Having this boundary set from the beginning will ensure that it does not cause an unnecessary argument later on in the relationship.

THOUGHT-PROVOKING QUOTE: "Boundaries are a prerequisite for intimacy. They are the scaffolding that allows the relationship to grow." — *Dr. John Gottman*

SOURCE OF WISDOM: 1 Corinthians 14:40 (NIV): "But everything should be done in a fitting and orderly way."

THE WORK: Defining Our Perimeter

GOAL: Establish one clear, mutual boundary to protect the emotional safety of your marriage, defining the consequence of violation.

1. **Define the Threat:** Both partners identify one behavior, action, or external influence that most frequently erodes your connection or safety (e.g., bringing up old arguments, constant phone use). Agree on one target threat.

2. **The Boundary:** Create one clear, actionable rule for this threat (e.g., "We will not discuss finances when children are awake").

3. **The Consequence:** Both partners agree on and write down what happens when the boundary is violated (e.g., "The discussion ends immediately," "The phone is put away for 30 minutes").

REFLECTION SPACE

Our New Boundary:

_____

_____

_____

_____

The Consequence of Violating It:

_____

_____

_____

_____

Why this boundary creates safety for me (Partner A):

_____

_____

_____

_____

Why this boundary creates safety for me (Partner B):

_____

_____

_____

_____

Our Shared Takeaway (The immediate action we must take):

_____

_____

DAY 18: OUR COMMUNICATION NORMS

DAILY LESSON

DAY 18: OUR COMMUNICATION NORMS

Snippet from "Me to We" (Chp 5): You may agree to prioritize transparency and authenticity in your interactions, avoiding passive-aggressive behavior, sarcasm, or avoidance tactics. Establishing these norms early on and re-enforcing those behaviors will make it easier and easier to naturally do them when conflicts arise in the future.

THOUGHT-PROVOKING QUOTE: "Shared laughter is the closest thing to shared communication." — *Karin Slaughter*

SOURCE OF WISDOM: Ephesians 4:29 (NIV): "Do not let any unwholesome talk come out of your mouths, but only what is helpful for building others up according to their needs, that it may benefit those who listen."

THE WORK: Creating Our Rules of Engagement

GOAL: Establish positive, proactive rules for how you will interact, especially when stressed or busy, avoiding passive-aggression.

1. **Norm #1 (Digital):** Both partners agree to and write down one rule for digital communication (e.g., "We will never use text message for emotional or conflict topics").

2. **Norm #2 (Verbal/Tone):** Both partners agree to and write down one rule for in-person communication (e.g., "We will not raise our voices above a level 7").

3. **The "Why":** Discuss how committing to these norms actively avoids a passive-aggressive reaction from your partner.

REFLECTION SPACE

Our First New Communication Norm (Digital) (Partner A writes):

_____

_____

_____

_____

Our First New Communication Norm (Digital) (Partner B writes):

_____

_____

_____

_____

Our Second New Communication Norm (Verbal/Tone) (Partner A writes):

_____

_____

_____

_____

Our Second New Communication Norm (Verbal/Tone) (Partner B writes):

_____

_____

_____

_____

Our Shared Takeaway (How these avoid passive-aggression):

_____

_____

DAY 19: FLEXIBILITY IN STYLE

DAILY LESSON

DAY 19: FLEXIBILITY IN STYLE

Snippet from "Me to We" (Chp 6): You and your partner must also recognize that communication styles may shift over time and in response to different situations. You may find that certain topics require a more nuanced approach or a higher level of sensitivity.

THOUGHT-PROVOKING QUOTE: "The measure of intelligence is the ability to change." — *Albert Einstein*

SOURCE OF WISDOM: Philippians 2:3-4 (NIV): "Do nothing out of selfish ambition or vain conceit, but in humility consider others better than yourselves. Each of you should look not only to your own interests, but also to the interests of others."

THE WORK: Adjusting for Empathy (Reciprocal)

GOAL: Both partners commit to adjusting their communication style as an act of love and respect for their partner's sensitivity on a specific topic.

1. **The Sensitive Topic:** Both partners identify one topic that causes their partner to immediately feel defensive (e.g., money, parenting style).

2. **The Adaptation:** Both partners write down one way they will adapt their approach next time they initiate that sensitive conversation with their partner (e.g., use less structured language, start with 3 compliments first).

3. **The Act of Love:** Both partners discuss why this adaptation is an act of humility and love.

REFLECTION SPACE

The Sensitive Topic for Partner B (Partner A identifies):

_____

_____

_____

_____

The Sensitive Topic for Partner A (Partner B identifies):

_____

_____

_____

_____

My Planned Style Adaptation for Partner B (Partner A writes):

_____

_____

_____

_____

My Planned Style Adaptation for Partner A (Partner B writes):

_____

_____

_____

_____

Our Shared Takeaway (Why this is an act of love):

_____

_____

DAY 20: THE DAILY CHECK-IN

DAILY LESSON

DAY 20: THE DAILY CHECK-IN

Snippet from "Me to We" (Chp 6): Establish a routine where you and your partner check in with each other daily. This regular practice fosters open communication and strengthens your connection.

THOUGHT-PROVOKING QUOTE: "The marriage is the daily, not the grand gesture." — *Mignon McLaughlin*

SOURCE OF WISDOM: Psalm 145:2 (NIV): "Every day I will bless you and extol your name forever and ever."

THE WORK: Practicing Presence

GOAL: Practice the structured Daily Check-In and define your joint plan for maintaining this routine.

1. **Establish a Routine:** Agree on a time and place today for a 10-minute check-in. Turn off all distractions.

2. **Practice:** Follow this three-part check-in structure: A) Share your "Highs and Lows" of the day. B) Express one piece of gratitude for the other person. C) Ask, "What do you need from me for the next 24 hours?"

3. **Commit:** Discuss the value of the routine and commit to doing this at least 5 times in the coming week.

REFLECTION SPACE

My High/Low for Today (Partner A):

_____

_____

_____

_____

My High/Low for Today (Partner B):

_____

_____

_____

_____

My Partner's Specific Need From Me (Partner A writes):

_____

_____

_____

_____

My Partner's Specific Need From Me (Partner B writes):

_____

_____

_____

_____

Our Shared Takeaway (Commitment Plan):

_____

_____

DAY 21: WEEK 3 REVIEW & GOAL SETTING

DAILY LESSON

DAY 21: WEEK 3 REVIEW & GOAL SETTING

Snippet from "Me to We" (Chp 5): Building consensus on communication norms and setting productive boundaries requires ongoing dialogue, mutual respect, and a commitment to understanding and honoring each other's needs and preferences.

THOUGHT-PROVOKING QUOTE: "Unity is strength... where there is teamwork and collaboration, wonderful things can be achieved." — *Mattie Stepanek*

SOURCE OF WISDOM: Romans 15:5-7 (NIV): "May the God who gives endurance and encouragement give you the same attitude of mind toward each other that Christ Jesus had... Accept one another, then, just as Christ accepted you, in order to bring praise to God."

THE WORK: The Unity Audit

GOAL: Identify the most powerful "Shared Language" rule and set a unified, reciprocal goal for navigating conflict in Week 4.

1. **The Unity Audit:** Review your new shared terms, boundaries, and norms. Both partners write down which "Shared Language" rule they believe will most improve your long-term connection.

2. **The Challenge:** Both partners write down the single greatest challenge or fear they face when conflict arises (e.g., Partner B shuts down, Partner A yells).

3. **The Goal:** Set one shared, measurable conflict-handling goal for Week 4 (e.g., "We will use the Time-Out cue once this week," or "We will not interrupt each other during a disagreement").

REFLECTION SPACE

The Most Impactful Shared Language Rule (Partner A):

_____

_____

_____

_____

The Most Impactful Shared Language Rule (Partner B):

_____

_____

_____

_____

My Greatest Conflict Fear (Partner A):

_____

_____

_____

_____

My Greatest Conflict Fear (Partner B):

_____

_____

_____

_____

Our Week 4 Conflict Goal:

_____

_____

WEEK 4: FROM CONFLICT TO CONNECTION (NAVIGATING CONSTRUCTIVELY)

DAY 22: CONFLICT AS OPPORTUNITY

DAILY LESSON

DAY 22: CONFLICT AS OPPORTUNITY

Snippet from "Me to We" (Chp 9): Acknowledge that misunderstandings may occur. View them as opportunities for growth and learning in your relationship.

THOUGHT-PROVOKING QUOTE: "Conflict is the beginning of consciousness." — *Carl Jung*

SOURCE OF WISDOM: James 1:2-4 (NIV): "Consider it pure joy, my brothers and sisters, whenever you face trials of many kinds, because you know that the testing of your faith produces perseverance."

THE WORK: The Deeper Message

GOAL: Both partners reframe a past disagreement by focusing on the underlying emotional need, not the superficial trigger.

1. **Reframe:** Briefly describe a past, unresolved conflict (e.g., "The fight about the lawn").

2. **The Deeper Message:** Both partners individually identify what the conflict *revealed* about their deeper needs or fears (e.g., "It wasn't about the lawn; it was about feeling like my home isn't valued").

3. **The Catalyst:** Discuss how this deeper revelation turns the conflict into a "catalyst for growth."

REFLECTION SPACE

The Underlying Fear/Deeper Need (Partner A):

_____

_____

_____

_____

The Underlying Fear/Deeper Need (Partner B):

_____

_____

_____

_____

My Partner's Deeper Message (What I heard) (Partner A writes):

_____

_____

_____

_____

My Partner's Deeper Message (What I heard) (Partner B writes):

_____

_____

_____

_____

Our Joint Growth Lesson:

_____

_____

DAY 23: COLLABORATIVE PROBLEM-SOLVING

DAILY LESSON

DAY 23: COLLABORATIVE PROBLEM-SOLVING

Snippet from "Me to We" (Chp 9): This may include discussing strategies for active listening, how to deliver constructive feedback, and what compromises might need to be made. They also commit to seeking solutions collaboratively and finding compromises that honor both parties' perspectives and preferences.

THOUGHT-PROVOKING QUOTE: "The greatest single source of relationship stability is the ability to communicate during conflict." — *Dr. John Gottman*

SOURCE OF WISDOM: Proverbs 15:22 (NIV): "Plans fail for lack of counsel, but with many advisers they succeed."

THE WORK: The 5-Step Resolution

GOAL: Practice resolving a disagreement using a structured, five-step collaborative process, highlighting the mutual compromise and skill used.

1. **Define the Problem:** Clearly state one current, moderate disagreement (e.g., who handles the evening routine).

2. **Brainstorm:** Spend 5 minutes generating solutions *without judgment* (Partner A list 3, Partner B list 3).

3. **Evaluate & Select:** Discuss the pros and cons of each solution and select one that honors both parties' core needs (the "we").

4. **The Skill:** Both partners write down the specific communication skill (Active Listening, "I" Statements, Boundary Setting) that made the final resolution possible.

REFLECTION SPACE

The Final Collaborative Solution:

_____

_____

_____

_____

What I Compromised (Partner A):

_____

_____

_____

_____

What I Compromised (Partner B):

_____

_____

_____

_____

The Skill That Made It Possible (Partner A):

_____

_____

_____

_____

The Skill That Made It Possible (Partner B):

_____

_____

_____

_____

DAY 24: EMOTIONAL FLOODING & PAUSING

DAILY LESSON

DAY 24: EMOTIONAL FLOODING & PAUSING

Snippet from "Me to We" (Chp 9): Being able to adjust to changing circumstances and navigate challenges with grace and compassion strengthens the bond between us and our partner. You may need to adjust your communication style to ensure that your message is conveyed respectfully and sensitively.

THOUGHT-PROVOKING QUOTE: "Between stimulus and response there is a space. In that space is our power to choose our response. In our response lies our growth and our freedom." — *Viktor Frankl*

SOURCE OF WISDOM: Proverbs 29:11 (NIV): "Fools give full vent to their rage, but the wise hold it in check."

THE WORK: The Time-Out Agreement

GOAL: Both partners create a mutual, non-verbal signal and a rule to prevent emotional flooding from derailing a constructive conversation.

1. **Define Flooding:** Both partners describe how they *feel* when they are emotionally flooded (e.g., heart races, can't think clearly, want to yell).

2. **The Cue:** Agree on a non-verbal cue (e.g., a hand signal, a phrase like "I need 10 to reset") for when one partner feels overwhelmed.

3. **The Respect:** Both partners write down why respecting the pause is an act of trust and love.

REFLECTION SPACE

My Feeling When Flooded (Partner A):

_____

_____

_____

_____

My Feeling When Flooded (Partner B):

_____

_____

_____

_____

Our Agreed-Upon Non-Verbal Cue & Pause Time:

_____

_____

_____

_____

Why respecting the pause is an act of trust (Partner A writes):

_____

_____

_____

_____

Why respecting the pause is an act of trust (Partner B writes):

_____

_____

_____

_____

DAY 25: THE FORGIVENESS CYCLE

DAILY LESSON

DAY 25: THE FORGIVENESS CYCLE

Snippet from "Me to We" (Chp 7): We are less apt to assume and more open to thinking out the possibilities, thus allowing us to reflect on the meaning before responding. Ultimately, building a strong and lasting partnership requires ongoing effort, patience, and dedication from both of you.

THOUGHT-PROVOKING QUOTE: "Forgiveness means giving up your right to hurt me for hurting you." — *Lewis B. Smedes*

SOURCE OF WISDOM: Matthew 6:14 (NIV): "For if you forgive other people when they sin against you, your heavenly Father will also forgive you."

THE WORK: Trust vs. Forgiveness

GOAL: Differentiate between the emotional act of forgiveness and the rational act of rebuilding trust, defining the action needed for the latter.

1. **Forgiveness Defined:** Both partners describe a resentment you have *already* released. Articulate the difference between forgiving (letting go of your own hurt) and trusting (requiring a demonstration of changed behavior).

2. **The Trust Gap:** Both partners identify one small area where trust still needs rebuilding from the other partner. What is the one specific action required to rebuild it?

3. **The Commitment:** Both partners commit to the next step.

REFLECTION SPACE

A Resentment I Fully Released (Partner A):

_____

_____

_____

_____

A Resentment I Fully Released (Partner B):

_____

_____

_____

_____

The Action I Need to See to Rebuild Trust (Partner A writes):

_____

_____

_____

_____

The Action I Need to See to Rebuild Trust (Partner B writes):

_____

_____

_____

_____

Our Shared Takeaway (Next Trust-Building Step):

_____

_____

DAY 26: REPAIR ATTEMPTS

DAILY LESSON

DAY 26: REPAIR ATTEMPTS

Snippet from "Me to We" (Chp 9): This simple yet powerful exercise reminds you of the positive aspects of your relationship and reinforces gratitude and love. You will form a deeper connection and navigate communication challenges with greater ease and empathy.

THOUGHT-PROVOKING QUOTE: "The smallest effort is not lost. Every experience is a success in its own right." — *Pema Chödrön*

SOURCE OF WISDOM: Galatians 6:1 (NIV): "Brothers and sisters, if someone is caught in a sin, you who live by the Spirit should restore that person gently."

THE WORK: Recognizing Restoration

GOAL: Both partners recognize and actively receive their partner's unique way of attempting to "repair" the relationship after conflict.

1. **Identify:** Both partners write down their partner's *most frequent* way of attempting to "repair" the relationship after a fight (e.g., a hug, making a joke, a simple "I'm sorry").

2. **The Resistance:** Both partners discuss and write down why that repair attempt sometimes *doesn't* work for them (e.g., "The joke feels like avoidance," or "The hug feels too soon").

3. **The Commitment:** Both commit to *actively valuing* their partner's repair attempt next time.

REFLECTION SPACE

My Partner's Most Frequent Repair Attempt (Partner A writes):

_____
_____
_____
_____

My Partner's Most Frequent Repair Attempt (Partner B writes):

_____
_____
_____
_____

Why that Attempt Sometimes Fails for Me (Partner A):

_____
_____
_____
_____

Why that Attempt Sometimes Fails for Me (Partner B):

_____
_____
_____
_____

Our Shared Takeaway (Commitment to Receiving):

_____
_____

DAY 27: RELATIONSHIP VISION

DAILY LESSON

DAY 27: RELATIONSHIP VISION

Snippet from "Me to We" (Chp 8): Create a vision board together that represents your shared goals, values, and aspirations as a couple. This activity strengthens your bond and reinforces your commitment to each other's happiness and fulfillment.

THOUGHT-PROVOKING QUOTE: "Where there is no vision, the people perish." — *Proverbs 29:18*

SOURCE OF WISDOM: Jeremiah 29:11 (NIV): "For I know the plans I have for you," declares the Lord, "plans to prosper you and not to harm you, plans to give you hope and a future."

THE WORK: Future Focus

GOAL: Both partners define a shared vision for your marriage's communication over the next year to guide your actions.

1. **The Vision:** Both partners individually complete this sentence: "One year from now, our communication will be characterized by..." (e.g., "mutual calm," "more laughter").

2. **The Milestones:** Both partners list two specific communication milestones you will track in the next year (e.g., a 3-hour phone-free date once a month, 100% successful Time-Outs during conflict).

3. **The "We" Identity:** Create a three-word motto for your marriage's communication style (e.g., "Gentle, Honest, Present").

REFLECTION SPACE

My Vision Statement (Partner A):

_____

_____

_____

_____

My Vision Statement (Partner B):

_____

_____

_____

_____

The Milestones I Will Commit To Tracking (Partner A):

_____

_____

_____

_____

The Milestones I Will Commit To Tracking (Partner B):

_____

_____

_____

_____

Our Three-Word Motto:

_____

_____

DAY 28: THE FINAL STEP: MUTUAL COMMITMENT

DAILY LESSON

DAY 28: THE FINAL STEP: MUTUAL COMMITMENT

Snippet from "Me to We" (Appendix): By prioritizing empathy, communication, and mutual respect, you will be able to create a relationship that is built to last: a partnership grounded in love, trust, and honesty.

THOUGHT-PROVOKING QUOTE: "Ultimately, the bond of all companionship, whether in marriage or in friendship, is conversation." — *Oscar Wilde*

SOURCE OF WISDOM: Hebrews 10:23-24 (NIV): "Let us hold unswervingly to the hope we profess, for he who promised is faithful. And let us consider how we may spur one another on toward love and good deeds."

THE WORK: Our Renewed Vows

GOAL: Both partners individually summarize their renewed commitment to communicating with emotional depth and affirm their partner's commitment.

1. **Vows Revisited:** Both partners individually write one sentence summarizing their renewed commitment to communicating with emotional depth.

2. **Read Aloud:** Read your commitment sentence to each other.

3. **Affirmation:** Both partners write down how that commitment will make them feel (e.g., "Your commitment to speaking your truth makes me feel safe and respected").

REFLECTION SPACE

My Renewed Commitment Sentence (Partner A):

_____

_____

_____

_____

My Renewed Commitment Sentence (Partner B):

_____

_____

_____

_____

My Affirmation of Partner B's Commitment (Partner A writes):

_____

_____

_____

_____

My Affirmation of Partner A's Commitment (Partner B writes):

_____

_____

_____

_____

Our Shared Takeaway (The Next Big Step):

_____

_____

SYNTHESIS & CELEBRATION

DAY 29: REVIEW & INTEGRATE

DAILY LESSON

DAY 29: REVIEW & INTEGRATE

Snippet from "Me to We" (Chp 10): The journey of building a strong and lasting partnership is a dynamic and multifaceted endeavor that requires dedication, effort, and mutual understanding from both partners.

THOUGHT-PROVOKING QUOTE: "We are what we repeatedly do. Excellence, then, is not an act, but a habit." — *Will Durant (paraphrasing Aristotle)*

SOURCE OF WISDOM: Deuteronomy 5:33 (NIV): "Walk in obedience to all that the Lord your God has commanded you, so that you may live and prosper and prolong your days in the land that you will possess."

THE WORK: The Habits of a Healthy Marriage

GOAL: Both partners identify the most impactful lessons and create a clear, unified plan for maintaining your new communication habits.

1. **Top 5:** Review your workbook notes from the past 4 weeks. Both partners individually identify the top 3 most impactful lessons you learned.

2. **Maintenance Plan:** Discuss and agree on a plan for how you will consistently maintain the most important practice (e.g., "We will do the Daily Check-In every evening").

3. **Success Measurement:** Both partners write down one single action you will track to prove your communication has improved in the next 30 days.

REFLECTION SPACE

My Top 3 Impactful Lessons (Partner A):

_____

_____

_____

_____

My Top 3 Impactful Lessons (Partner B):

_____

_____

_____

_____

Our Plan for Maintenance (The New Habit We Will Stick To):

_____

_____

_____

_____

My Success Measurement Action (Partner A):

_____

_____

_____

_____

My Success Measurement Action (Partner B):

_____

_____

_____

_____

DAY 30: THE MUTUAL REWARD PAYOFF

DAILY LESSON

DAY 30: THE MUTUAL REWARD PAYOFF

Snippet from "Me to We" (Chp 10): By establishing a sense of unity and cohesion within the relationship, you and your partner will craft a unified identity and direction, strengthen your connection through mutual understanding, and align your goals and visions for the future.

THOUGHT-PROVOKING QUOTE: "Love does not consist of gazing at each other, but in looking outward together in the same direction." — *Antoine de Saint-Exupéry*

SOURCE OF WISDOM: 1 Corinthians 13:13 (NIV): "And now these three remain: faith, hope and love. But the greatest of these is love."

THE WORK: The Empathy Exam & Payoff

GOAL: Fulfill your 30-day contract and use the reward exchange as a final test of empathy and attention to your partner's needs.

1. **The Contract Reveal:** Open the sealed Mutual Reward Contract from Day 1. Exchange the original commitment notes (the rewards you promised each other).

2. **The Empathy Exam:** Complete the Reflection Space below. Your goal is to see how well you *truly* know your partner now, versus what you *thought* they wanted 30 days ago.

3. **The Payoff:** Agree on a date for both rewards to be redeemed. Then, open the Appreciation Jar (from Day 14) and read the notes aloud. Celebrate the strength of your new shared language!

REFLECTION SPACE

My Partner's Sealed Commitment (What Partner B wrote on Day 1) (Partner A reads):

_____

_____

_____

_____

My Partner's Sealed Commitment (What Partner A wrote on Day 1) (Partner B reads):

_____

_____

_____

_____

My Reflection on My Own Commitment (Did it still match my partner's need?) (Partner A):

_____

_____

_____

_____

My Reflection on My Own Commitment (Did it still match my partner's need?) (Partner B):

_____

_____

_____

_____

Our Next 30-Day Communication Goal:

_____

_____

THE BEGINNING OF "WE" 💍

Congratulations! You have reached the end of the 30-Day Workbook.

If you have completed the journey with commitment and honesty, you have done more for your relationship in the last four weeks than most couples do in a year. You have faced vulnerability, embraced discomfort, and demonstrated the deepest kind of love: the willingness to do the hard work for the sake of the **"We."**

The Mutual Reward Contract has been opened, the rewards have been scheduled, but the true payoff is in the **shared language** you now possess.

The Three Pillars of Your New Foundation

As you move forward, your communication will stand on these three pillars, which you built in the past 30 days:

1. **I Know My "Me" Factor:** You have defined your core needs, acknowledged your communication heritage, and converted hidden expectations into clear, actionable requests. You speak with **I-Statements**, not global attacks.

2. **We Own Our Shared Language:** You have defined your key terms, created mutual boundaries (**The Perimeter**), and agreed upon your **Rules of Engagement** for both verbal and digital communication. You have a dictionary that is unique to your marriage.

3. **We Master the Repair:** You no longer fear conflict because you have a plan. You know how to identify emotional flooding (using **The Time-Out Agreement**), you know how to apologize with sincerity, and you understand that conflict is merely a catalyst for deeper understanding.

THE COMMITMENT: FROM PRACTICE TO HABIT

The journey from "Me" to "We" is not a 30-day course; it is a **lifetime practice.** Your success now depends entirely on maintenance.

YOUR LIFELONG CHALLENGE:

1. **Maintain the Check-In:** Commit to the **Daily Check-In** (Day 20) for the next 90 days. Non-negotiable, phone-free, 10 minutes. This routine is your insurance policy against communication drift.

2. **Review the Blueprint:** Go back to your notes and look at the **Boundaries** (Day 17) and the **Rules of Engagement** (Day 18). Schedule a quarterly (every 90 days) review to discuss any rules that need adjusting.

3. **Use Your Motto:** Remember your three-word motto from Day 27 (e.g., *Gentle, Honest, Present*). When stress hits, speak that motto aloud to yourself or your partner to instantly reset the conversation.

The Next Step in Your Journey

To keep your skills sharp and continue the momentum, the next step is to make your practice fun and systematic.

Keep the work going with the games:

Thank you for choosing to invest in your relationship. Now go forth, communicate with grace, and enjoy the **"We"** you have built together.
Eric A. Williams, Ph.D.

[Insert Final Reflection/Signature Space Here]

APPENDIX

APPENDIX A:
30-DAY WORKBOOK EXERCISE REFERENCE

This reference guide provides a concise summary of the daily exercises, including the goal and steps for each partner, to help orient you to the structure and content of the "Me" to "We" journey.

WEEK 1: THE "ME" FACTOR (UNDERSTANDING MY COMMUNICATION BLUEPRINT)

Day	Exercise Title	Goal & Steps (The Work)
Day 1	Our Mutual Reward Contract	GOAL: Establish the positive incentive that will power you through the next 30 days as a unified team. Steps: 1. Write down one specific, memorable reward (Act of Service/Quality Time) for your partner, without sharing. 2. Sign and date the commitment. 3. Seal the contract to be opened on Day 30.
Day 2	Map It: Our Communication Heritage	GOAL: Uncover unconscious communication habits inherited from your families of origin. Steps: 1. Both partners chart 3 distinct family communication "rules." 2. Discuss the feeling your partner's top rule triggers in you. 3. Agree on one mutual communication rule to retire from your marriage.

Day 3	Listing Our Core Needs	GOAL: Clearly articulate your top three emotional needs and commit to meeting one of your partner's needs. Steps: 1. Both partners list their top 3 core emotional needs and discuss the most urgent one. 2. Both partners write down one specific, small way they will try to meet the other partner's *most urgent* need in the next 48 hours.
Day 4	Unpacking the Hidden	GOAL: Bring one uncommunicated expectation into the light and convert it into a direct, healthy request. Steps: 1. Both partners write down one *uncommunicated* expectation. 2. Write down the emotional reaction when this expectation goes unmet. 3. Rephrase the expectation as a clear, loving, and actionable direct request.

Day 5	Assessing Our Aim (Reciprocal)	GOAL: Reciprocally assess the communication "Arrow" used during conflict and commit to aiming for the Effective Arrow. Steps: 1. Partner A describes a disagreement; Partner B assesses the "Arrow" (e.g., Toxic, Passive, Effective) used. 2. Swap roles (B describes, A assesses). 3. Jointly identify one specific change to aim for the Effective Arrow next time.
Day 6	The "I" Statement Challenge	GOAL: Practice expressing feelings and needs without using global attacks or "All-or-Nothing" phrases. Steps: 1. Both partners write down one "All-or-Nothing" phrase they use or hear. 2. Both partners rephrase the phrase into a constructive "I" statement. 3. Share the "I" statements and commit to using them going forward.

Day 7	The "Me" Audit and "We" Focus	GOAL: Summarize individual lessons from Week 1 and set a unified goal for the next week.
		Steps: 1. Discuss one thing learned about your *own* communication style this week.
		2. Write down how this self-knowledge changes how you will listen to your partner.
		3. Set one shared communication goal for Week 2 (e.g., focusing on Love Languages).

WEEK 2: DECODING OUR LANGUAGES (LOVE, APOLOGY, AND STYLE)

Day	Exercise Title	Goal & Steps (The Work)
Day 8	The Language Gap (Reciprocal)	GOAL: Confirm your Love Language and identify where a recent effort missed the mark. Steps: 1. Both partners clearly state their primary Love Language. 2. Both describe a time their partner showed love using a *different* language. 3. Write one specific way to ensure your next effort lands correctly.
Day 9	Intentional Practice	GOAL: Apply intentional effort to serve your partner using their specific Love Language today. Steps: 1. Both partners commit to one small, intentional act that aligns *perfectly* with their partner's Love Language today. 2. Report on the emotional impact of the received act. 3. Rate the emotional connection on a scale of 1-10.

Day 10	The Anatomy of Our Apologies	GOAL: Identify your natural apology style and commit to integrating the Accepting Responsibility language. Steps: 1. Write a brief apology and analyze which of the 5 Apology Languages you naturally lean toward. 2. Exchange and review apologies, discussing if the partner's style felt satisfying. 3. Commit to intentionally integrating the Accepting Responsibility language into your next apology.
Day 11	Defining "Sincere"	GOAL: Define what a genuine repair attempt looks and feels like to you. Steps: 1. Both partners explain what a true, sincere apology looks and feels like to them (words, tone, behavior). 2. Describe a past argument where the apology felt superficial and what was missing. 3. Agree on a phrase your partner can use when an apology feels incomplete.

Day 12	Assertiveness in Practice	GOAL: Practice asserting a need clearly and respectfully, shifting away from passive or aggressive communication. Steps: 1. Identify one moment this week where you felt Passive and one where you felt Aggressive. 2. Rewrite the passive moment using a clear, respectful "I" Statement to assert the original need. 3. Practice the rewritten assertive statements aloud.
Day 13	Silent Signals (Reciprocal)	GOAL: Practice observation and decoding the unspoken language of the body and tone. Steps: 1. Partner A speaks for 3 minutes (neutral topic); Partner B silently observes and decodes non-verbal cues. 2. Swap roles. 3. Confirm the accuracy of the reading and discuss which non-verbal cue is the most dominant signal in your marriage.

Day 14	The Appreciation Jar & The "We" Goal	GOAL: Focus on gratitude and set a goal for building your shared language in Week 3. Steps: 1. Both partners write down three specific ways their partner demonstrated understanding of their "languages" this week. 2. Read them to your partner. 3. Set one shared communication goal for Week 3: Crafting Our "We" (e.g., "We will define one common word that causes confusion").

WEEK 3: CRAFTING OUR "WE" (BUILDING THE SHARED LANGUAGE)

Day	Exercise Title	Goal & Steps (The Work)
Day 15	Defining Our Dictionary	GOAL: Negotiate and agree on precise, shared definitions for two words that often lead to miscommunication. Steps: 1. List two words or phrases that have consistently caused confusion (e.g., "Clean the house"). 2. Both partners write down their individual definitions for Term 1. 3. Negotiate and write down one precise, shared definition for Term 1 to commit to using.
Day 16	The 3-Minute Mirror (Reciprocal)	GOAL: Practice the core skill of reflective listening to ensure comprehension before response. Steps: 1. Partner A speaks for 3 minutes on a challenge; Partner B must then reflect back (paraphrase) exactly what they heard. 2. Swap roles. 3. Both partners write about their success in reflection and how it felt to be fully heard.

Day 17	Defining Our Perimeter	GOAL: Establish one clear, mutual boundary to protect the emotional safety of your marriage. Steps: 1. Both partners identify one threat that most frequently erodes your connection. 2. Create one clear, actionable Boundary (e.g., "We will not discuss finances when children are awake"). 3. Agree on and write down the Consequence when the boundary is violated.
Day 18	Creating Our Rules of Engagement	GOAL: Establish positive, proactive rules for how you will interact, especially when stressed. Steps: 1. Agree on and write down one rule for digital communication (e.g., "No emotional topics via text"). 2. Agree on and write down one rule for verbal/tone (e.g., "We will not raise our voices above a level 7"). 3. Discuss how committing to these norms avoids a passive-aggressive reaction.

Day 19	Adjusting for Empathy (Reciprocal)	GOAL: Commit to adjusting your communication style as an act of love for your partner's sensitivity on a specific topic. Steps: 1. Both partners identify one topic that causes their partner to immediately feel defensive. 2. Write down one way you will adapt your approach next time you initiate that conversation. 3. Discuss why this adaptation is an act of humility and love.
Day 20	Practicing Presence	GOAL: Practice the structured Daily Check-In and define your joint plan for maintaining this routine. Steps: 1. Agree on a time and place for a 10-minute check-in; turn off distractions. 2. Practice the three-part check-in: Highs/ Lows, Gratitude, and "What do you need from me for the next 24 hours?" 3. Commit to doing this at least 5 times in the coming week.

Day 21	The Unity Audit	GOAL: Set a unified, reciprocal goal for navigating conflict in Week 4.
		Steps: 1. Both partners write down which "Shared Language" rule (from Week 3) they believe will most improve your long-term connection.
		2. Both partners write down the single greatest challenge or fear they face when conflict arises.
		3. Set one shared, measurable conflict-handling goal for Week 4.

WEEK 4: FROM CONFLICT TO CONNECTION (NAVIGATING CONSTRUCTIVELY)

Day	Exercise Title	Goal & Steps (The Work)
Day 22	The Deeper Message	GOAL: Reframe a past disagreement by focusing on the underlying emotional need, not the superficial trigger. Steps: 1. Briefly describe a past, unresolved conflict (e.g., "The fight about the budget"). 2. Both partners individually identify what the conflict *revealed* about their deeper needs or fears (e.g., "I need security"). 3. Discuss how this deeper revelation turns the conflict into a "catalyst for growth."
Day 23	The 5-Step Resolution	GOAL: Practice resolving a disagreement using a structured, five-step collaborative process. Steps: 1. Define one current, moderate disagreement. 2. Brainstorm solutions *without judgment*. 3. Select one solution that honors both parties' core needs. 4. Both partners write down the specific communication skill that made the final resolution possible.

Day 24	The Time-Out Agreement	GOAL: Create a mutual, non-verbal signal and a rule to prevent emotional flooding. Steps: 1. Both partners describe how they *feel* when they are emotionally flooded. 2. Agree on a non-verbal cue for when one partner feels overwhelmed (e.g., hand signal, "I need 10 to reset"). 3. Both partners write down why respecting the pause is an act of trust and love.
Day 25	Trust vs. Forgiveness	GOAL: Differentiate between the emotional act of forgiveness and the rational act of rebuilding trust. Steps: 1. Articulate the difference between forgiving (releasing the hurt) and trusting (requiring changed behavior). 2. Identify one small area where trust still needs rebuilding and the one specific action required from the other partner. 3. Both partners commit to the next step.

Day 26	Recognizing Restoration	GOAL: Actively receive your partner's unique way of attempting to "repair" the relationship after conflict. Steps: 1. Both partners write down their partner's *most frequent* way of attempting to "repair" the relationship (e.g., a hug, a joke, an apology). 2. Discuss and write down why that repair attempt sometimes *doesn't* work for you. 3. Both commit to *actively valuing* their partner's repair attempt next time.
Day 27	Future Focus	GOAL: Define a shared vision for your marriage's communication over the next year. Steps: 1. Both partners complete the sentence: "One year from now, our communication will be characterized by..." 2. List two specific communication milestones you will track in the next year. 3. Create a three-word motto for your marriage's communication style (e.g., "Gentle, Honest, Present").

Day 28	Our Renewed Vows	GOAL: Summarize your renewed commitment to communicating with emotional depth and affirm your partner's commitment. Steps: 1. Both partners individually write one sentence summarizing their renewed commitment. 2. Read your commitment sentence to each other. 3. Both partners write down how that commitment will make them feel.

SYNTHESIS & CELEBRATION

Day	Exercise Title	Goal & Steps (The Work)
Day 29	The Habits of a Healthy Marriage	GOAL: Identify the most impactful lessons and create a clear, unified plan for maintenance. Steps: 1. Both partners identify the top 3 most impactful lessons learned over the 4 weeks. 2. Discuss and agree on a plan for how you will consistently maintain the most important practice (e.g., the Daily Check-In). 3. Both partners write down one single action you will track to prove your communication has improved in the next 30 days.
Day 30	The Empathy Exam & Payoff	GOAL: Fulfill your 30-day contract and celebrate the journey. Steps: 1. Open the sealed Mutual Reward Contract from Day 1 and exchange the original commitment notes. 2. Complete the Reflection Space to compare your Day 1 commitment with your current understanding of your partner's needs. 3. Agree on a date for the rewards to be redeemed, and read the notes from the Appreciation Jar aloud.

APPENDIX B

STRATEGIES FOR WEEKS 1 & 2: DEFINING THE "ME"

These exercises focus on your individual experiences, needs, and communication habits. Be honest with yourself and avoid worrying about what your partner might think—that's the whole point of sharing!

Exercise	Strategy for Completion	Example
Day 2: Communication Heritage	**Focus on the Feeling:** Don't just list a rule (e.g., "We avoid conflict"). Focus on the emotional impact. If a family rule was to yell, the impact on you might be that you feel fear or shut down when conflict starts. **The Upgrade:** Turn the old rule into a simple, positive replacement.	**Old Rule (Partner A):** My family used sarcasm to manage stress. **The Impact (on Partner B):** When you get stressed and use sarcasm, I feel mocked and assume you don't respect my feelings, so I stop talking. **Rule to Retire:** Sarcasm is no longer a tool in our marriage.

| Day 4: Unpacking the Hidden | Uncover the "Shoulds": A hidden expectation is often a thought that begins with, "They should know…" or "They should do this because they love me." Convert this invisible "should" into a visible, respectful "I need" request. | Hidden Expectation: "My partner should spontaneously plan an anniversary dinner since I handle all the daily cooking."

The Consequence: "I feel unappreciated and sad when they don't plan special events."

The Direct Request (New Rule): "I need to feel celebrated for our anniversary, so please initiate planning a celebration at least one month in advance, or let me know if you'd like me to take the lead." |

Day 6: The "I" Statement Challenge	**Use the 3-Part Formula:** Every healthy "I" statement contains three parts: I feel (Emotion) + when (Behavior) + because (Need/Value). Avoid blaming words like always or never.	**Hidden Expectation:** "My partner should spontaneously plan an anniversary dinner since I handle all the daily cooking."
		The Consequence: "I feel unappreciated and sad when they don't plan special events."
		The Direct Request (New Rule): "I need to feel celebrated for our anniversary, so please initiate planning a celebration at least one month in advance, or let me know if you'd like me to take the lead."

Day 6: The "I" Statement Challenge	**Use the 3-Part Formula:** Every healthy "I" statement contains three parts: I feel (Emotion) + when (Behavior) + because (Need/Value). Avoid blaming words like always or never.	**Toxic Phrase:** "You never listen to me!" **The "I" Statement Rewrite:** "I feel unheard and lonely (Emotion) when you look at your phone while I'm sharing about my workday (Behavior), because I need to feel like I am your priority in that moment (Need)."
Day 10: The Anatomy of Our Apologies	**Listen for Their Need:** Your natural apology style (e.g., "Making Restitution" by buying flowers) might not match your partner's need (e.g., "Accepting Responsibility"). **The Goal:** Commit to verbally stating: "I accept full responsibility for [specific action]. I was wrong."	**Partner A's Natural Style:** Expressing Regret (saying, "I'm so sorry you're hurting"). **Partner B's Need:** Accepting Responsibility. **New Commitment:** When apologizing, I will first say, "I take responsibility for raising my voice. That was unacceptable, and I was wrong."

STRATEGIES FOR WEEK 3: CRAFTING OUR "WE"

These exercises require negotiation. Remember: **The goal is not to win the argument, but to achieve clarity.**

Exercise	Strategy for Completion	Example
Day 15: Defining Our Dictionary	**Quantify the Vague:** Vague words lead to conflict. Replace general terms with measurable ones. This applies to money, time, cleanliness, and chores.	**Confusing Term:** "Clean the house." **Partner A's Definition:** The kitchen counters are wiped, and the living room is vacuumed. **Partner B's Definition:** All dishes are put away, mail is sorted, and the bathroom mirror is wiped down. **Our Shared Definition:** "A 'clean house' means all dirty dishes are loaded, all surfaces in the kitchen and bathroom are wiped, and all mail has been taken off the kitchen counter."

Day 16: The 3-Minute Mirror	**Listen to Reflect, Not to Respond:** Your only job is to reflect back the speaker's core message and feeling. If they say, "I feel stressed about the kids' schedule," you should say: "What I hear you saying is that you're feeling a high level of stress right now, and the primary source of that stress is managing the kids' schedule." **(Do not offer a solution until the speaker confirms the reflection is correct).**	**Speaker (Partner A):** "I'm frustrated because I feel like I'm doing all the financial tracking by myself, and I'm anxious about our upcoming trip budget." **Reflector (Partner B):** "Okay, I hear two things: You feel frustrated and anxious because you feel like the entire burden of financial tracking is on your shoulders, and that's tied to the upcoming trip. Did I get that right?"

| Day 17: Defining Our Perimeter | **Set Boundaries Around Behavior:** A boundary is not a threat; it's a statement of what you will do to protect yourself or the relationship. It must be actionable by you. | **The Threat:** One of us brings up past hurts/arguments to win the current fight.

The Boundary: "We will not use any language that starts with 'Remember when you...' or 'You always...' during conflict."

The Consequence: "If that boundary is crossed, the non-violating partner will say, 'Boundary,' and the discussion immediately stops for 30 minutes so both of us can calm down." |

STRATEGIES FOR WEEK 4: CONFLICT TO CONNECTION

These exercises focus on navigating high-stress situations constructively. Your commitment to these rules is a commitment to the health of your future.

Exercise	Strategy for Completion	Example
Day 22: The Deeper Message	**Ask "Why Does This Matter to Me?"** The conflict is rarely about the dishes. It's about what the dishes represent. Keep asking "why" until you find the core need.	**Superficial Conflict:** The fight about the lawn being dead. **The Deeper Message:** "It wasn't about the dead lawn; it was about the fact that when things fall apart, I feel a loss of control (Partner A) and when you don't take charge, I feel like I have to carry the mental load for our image to others (Partner B)." **Joint Growth Lesson:** We learned Partner A needs to be more assertive about asking for help, and Partner B needs to view the home's maintenance as a shared symbol of our partnership.

Day 24: Emotional Flooding & Pausing	**Respect the Pause Time:** A "Time-Out" is useless if the pausing partner uses the time to plan their next attack, or if the waiting partner hovers and pressures them. The rule must be respected for the time and space it provides.	**Flooding Sign (Partner A):** My heart races, and I start shaking. **Agreed Cue:** The pausing partner says, "Time-Out: Reset," and holds up a closed fist. **The Rule (Commitment):** The pausing partner must promise to return to the discussion (e.g., "I will check in via text in 30 minutes to set a time to talk later"), and the waiting partner must not follow or continue the discussion in any way until that agreed-upon time.

Day 27: Future Focus	**Be Specific, Not Just Aspirational:** Your vision should be grounded in the skills you've learned. The goal isn't just "to be happier," but to define the behaviors that create happiness.	**Vague Vision:** To be happier. **Specific Vision:** "One year from now, our communication will be characterized by mutual calm, quick repairs after conflict, and five minutes of phone-free conversation every morning." **Three-Word Motto:** Gentle, Honest, Present. (Use your motto as a quick check when things get stressful.)

www.ingramcontent.com/pod-product-compliance
Lightning Source LLC
Chambersburg PA
CBHW052116020426
42335CB00021B/2785